YOU CHOOSE

GREAT ESCAPES

CAN YOU SURVIVE A REVOLUTIONARY WAR ESCAPE?

AN INTERACTIVE HISTORY ADVENTURE

BY BLAKE HOENA

CAPSTONE PRESS
a capstone imprint

Published by Capstone Press, an imprint of Capstone
1710 Roe Crest Drive, North Mankato, Minnesota 56003
capstonepub.com

Library of Congress Cataloging-in-Publication Data
Names: Hoena, B. A., author.
Title: Can you survive a Revolutionary War escape? : an interactive history adventure / by Blake Hoena.
Description: North Mankato, Minnesota : Capstone Press, 2024. | Series: You choose: great escapes | Includes bibliographical references. | Audience: Ages 8–12. | Audience: Grades 4–6. | Summary: An interactive Revolutionary War adventure where the reader is cornered by the British and their plot choices determine whether they make it out alive.
Identifiers: LCCN 2023023842 (print) | LCCN 2023023843 (ebook) | ISBN 9781669061267 (hardback) | ISBN 9781669061366 (paperback) | ISBN 9781669061304 (pdf) | ISBN 9781669061373 (epub)
Subjects: LCSH: Plot-your-own stories. | CYAC: United States—History—Revolution, 1775-1783—Fiction. | Plot-your-own stories. | LCGFT: Choose-your-own stories. | Novels.
Classification: LCC PZ7.H67127 Cam 2024 (print) | LCC PZ7.H67127 (ebook) | DDC [Fic]—dc23
LC record available at https://lccn.loc.gov/2023023842
LC ebook record available at https://lccn.loc.gov/2023023843

Editorial Credits
Editor: Christopher Harbo; Designer: Sarah Bennett; Media Researcher: Svetlana Zhurkin; Production Specialist: Katy LaVigne

Image Credits
Alamy: Niday Picture Library, 103, North Wind Picture Archives, 32, 45, 55, 105, Science History Images, cover, 62; DVIC: NARA, 38; Getty Images: mikroman6, 92, MPI, 17; Library of Congress: 9, 22, 25, 42, 59, 78, 102; Line of Battle Enterprise: 6, 12, 35; The New York Public Library: The Miriam and Ira D. Wallach Division of Art/Prints and Photographs, 21, 74, 84, 97; Shutterstock: holwichaikawee (jail background), cover, back cover and throughout, knyazevfoto, 71, Morphart Creation, 89, Nik Merkulov (grunge background), 6 and throughout; Smithsonian Institution: National Portrait Gallery/partial gift of Mr. Lawrence A. Fleischman, 82; Superstock: Everett Collection, 100, Steve Vidler, 40; The U.S. National Guard: 30; XNR Productions: 106

Printed and bound in China. 6274

CONTENTS

ABOUT YOUR ADVENTURE

YOU are fighting for the American colonies during the Revolutionary War (1775–1783). While bravely battling for independence, you get cornered by the British. Will you find a way to escape their clutches and fight another day for the new country you are trying to help create?

Chapter One sets the scene. Then you choose which path to read. Follow the directions at the bottom of the page as you read the stories. The decisions you make will change your outcome. After you finish one path, go back and read the others for new perspectives and more adventures.

Turn the page to begin your adventure.

The first shots of the Revolutionary War were fired at the Battles of Lexington and Concord, west of Boston, Massachusetts.

CHAPTER 1

THE FIGHT FOR INDEPENDENCE

On April 19, 1775, you heard what had happened. The previous night, a group of British Redcoats had left Boston, Massachusetts, and marched toward the town of Concord. The colonists were rumored to be hiding weapons there, and British troops had been ordered to seize them.

What happened next would change the lives of everyone in the Thirteen Colonies. Farmers and shop owners throughout the area took up arms. These militia gathered by the hundreds to face the British in the Battles of Lexington and Concord.

Turn the page.

You did not take part in the fighting, but you heard of the militia's victory. News of it spread quickly throughout the colonies. The Redcoats were driven back to Boston. It was a cause for celebration.

It was also a reason to worry. You know this minor skirmish will have major consequences for the colonists. The British won't let an act of rebellion against their authority go unpunished.

But you also hear rumblings from unhappy colonists. Many were already about to rebel. They felt British laws and taxes were unfair. After the shots fired that spring day, many more are now inspired to revolt. The Battles of Lexington and Concord signal the start of a much bigger conflict. The colonists' fight for independence from Great Britain in what will become known as the Revolutionary War has begun!

In the coming days and weeks, you hear that leaders throughout the colonies are gathering in Philadelphia, Pennsylvania. They form the Second Continental Congress. This group of Founders is in charge of governing the colonies and preparing them for war. One of their first acts is to establish the Continental Army. They place George Washington from Virginia in command.

The Continental Congress chose George Washington to lead the Continental Army because of his military experience in the French and Indian War (1754–1763).

Turn the page.

You are encouraged by this bit of news. During the French and Indian War, Washington proved to be a capable leader.

You know the colonists will be up against one of the world's greatest powers. The British Redcoats are well-armed and professionally trained. The colonies will need all the help they can muster. So you decide to join the Patriots in their fight for independence.

But how will you serve?

You could be an officer in the Continental Army and serve as an advisor to General Washington. It would be an honor to serve alongside a hero of the French and Indian War.

You could serve as a sailor. You would be fighting against the mighty British Royal Navy. Your mind swirls with excitement just thinking of the adventures you might have at sea.

Or you could serve in the southern colonies. While the fighting began in the New England area to the north, the war will spread throughout the colonies. The colonists in the south need to prepare for the battles ahead—and you could be instrumental to their success.

No matter the choice you make, there will be danger. You will face death and risk being captured by the Redcoats.

To advise General Washington, turn to page 13.
To sail with the Continental Navy, turn to page 41.
To join forces fighting in the south, turn to page 79.

George Washington was 43 years old when he became Commander in Chief of the Continental Army.

CHAPTER 2

THE BATTLE OF LONG ISLAND

You decide to join George Washington. The fight for independence will be a difficult one, and he will need the advice of trusted officers such as yourself to defeat the British.

In the summer of 1775, you march with him toward Boston. Shortly after the Battles of Lexington and Concord, colonial forces surrounded the city. But Boston was very well-defended, and the colonial army was only a ragtag bunch of volunteers. They also did not have the means to stop British supply ships from reaching Boston.

Turn the page.

The Siege of Boston is at a stalemate when you arrive with Washington. Upon taking command of the forces surrounding the city, he intensifies the attacks on British positions. Then in the spring of 1776, you watch as the Redcoats under the command of British General William Howe sail out of Boston Harbor.

While the soldiers of the Continental Army celebrate the victory, Washington meets with his officers. He knows this is just one small victory in a long war. He is already anticipating Howe's next move.

"I fear the British will set their sights on New York," Washington tells his officers as he points to the city on a map.

"But they sailed north from Boston," an officer replies, motioning to a spot farther north. "We have reports General Howe is now in Halifax."

Looking at the map, you see the officer is pointing to the Province of Nova Scotia. It's far from New York City. But you understand Washington's concern. Not only is New York a major trading hub, but it is also centrally located.

"As soon as the British regroup, they'll be on the move," Washington says. "We must be ready."

"And if they take New York, they could cut the colonies in half," you add. "That would make this war ever more difficult to win."

Washington gives you a nod of approval. Soon all the other officers are in agreement. But what you do not know is that Washington's decision to defend New York City will lead to one of the greatest escapes of the Revolutionary War!

In April 1776, Washington marches the Continental Army to New York. He has nearly 20,000 soldiers under his command.

Turn the page.

"I believe the British will focus their attack on Manhattan, the city's main island," Washington says at a meeting of his officers. He goes on to say that he will oversee the Army's main force on the southern tip of the island. He is also sending a division of soldiers, under the command of Brigadier General Nathanael Greene, across the East River to Long Island. The defense there will keep the British from sailing up the East River to the northern reaches of Manhattan.

Then Washington asks you whether you would prefer to join Greene in fortifying the defenses on Long Island or stay in Manhattan to prepare for the British attack. Both are equally worthy assignments.

To go to Long Island with Greene, go to page 17.
To stay in Manhattan with Washington, turn to page 20.

Brigadier General Nathanael Greene

You offer to assist Greene. With Washington in charge of the troops on Manhattan, you know they are in good hands. But the defenses on Long Island will be important to maintain control of the city. Artillery stationed in forts along the East River will prevent British ships from sailing up the river. If British troops were to reach northern Manhattan, they could trap the forces under General Washington's command on the island. That would spell disaster. The Continental Army would be forced to surrender, and the war could be over before it truly began.

Turn the page.

The main forts on Long Island defend Brooklyn Heights. That is where you are on June 29, 1776, when warning signals tell of the arrival of the British. They land on Staten Island, which is south of Long Island.

The Continental Army does not have the ships to challenge the Royal Navy. All you can do is continue to fortify your defenses and wait. You wait as more and more British ships arrive. There are hundreds of them carrying tens of thousands of Redcoats.

"Looks like all of London afloat out in the bay," you hear one soldier remark.

You continue to wait until August 22 when several thousand British troops land on Long Island, just miles from your position.

"We must go on the offensive," one officer tells Greene, "and push the Redcoats into the sea."

"But orders were to fortify our positions," another officer pipes in.

Greene looks pale and feverish as he asks your opinion. You know an attack could keep the British from bringing more troops to the island. If they aren't stopped, they will eventually outnumber your forces. But then again, your orders were to build up the defenses on the island. They are meant to protect your troops from the warships out in the bay.

To attack the British on Long Island, turn to page 22.
To continue working on the defenses, turn to page 25.

You decide to stay with Washington in Manhattan. It is where you believe the main fighting will take place. Then on June 29, 1776, warning signals sound. British ships are spotted approaching Staten Island to the south. Washington was correct in anticipating that General Howe would attack New York. You assume he will also be correct about where the British will direct their attack on the city.

Over the coming weeks, more and more British ships arrive. The count tops 400, and you guess that their forces will outnumber the Continental Army by the time the fighting begins.

Then on August 22, the British make their move. They land troops on Long Island.

"I think it's a ruse," Washington says. "Reports say they sent fewer than 10,000 troops."

The British fleet in Lower New York Bay before the Battle of Long Island

"But if they take Long Island, we can't stop their ships from sailing up the East River," an officer adds. "They could easily surround us."

Then Washington turns to you. Do you suggest moving more troops to Long Island? They could be needed to protect the forts there from the invading British. Or do you agree with Washington? Do you tell him that protecting Manhattan is the key to defending New York?

To send more troops to Long Island, turn to page 24.
To keep troops on Manhattan, turn to page 27.

British ships in Lower New York Bay were easily spotted from the hills of Long Island.

"We shouldn't give the British time to land more troops on the island," you say. "Let's attack!"

But then another officer pipes in, "What about the warships out in the bay? We would be unprotected from their cannons."

Greene coughs and then nods in agreement with the officer. The decision is made to defend the forts.

Over the next few days, you notice Greene becomes more and more feverish.

Then one morning he tells you, "I am being relieved of my command due to my illness. Washington has ordered you to join me."

You do not know whether this is a punishment for wanting to go against orders or whether Washington has other plans for you. You have no choice but to obey.

You leave with Greene. Your part in the Battle of Long Island has come to a disappointing end.

THE END

To read another adventure, turn to page 11.
To learn more about Revolutionary War escapes, turn to page 101.

"But what if it's not a ruse?" you say. "What if Howe plans to attack Long Island? Should those defenses fall, the British could sail up the East River and surround us. We'd be trapped!"

Washington thinks about what you say and agrees to send 1,500 more troops to Long Island.

"I am also placing Major General Israel Putnam in command on Long Island," Washington adds. "You will go with them to help oversee the defense."

You wonder if he is punishing you for disagreeing with him. However, you have no choice but to obey orders.

Turn to page 26.

"We must focus our efforts on the defenses," you say. "Plus, if we attack British positions on the island, we'd be in range of the cannons aboard their warships."

Greene wipes his brow and nods in agreement.

Over the coming days, more British troops land on the island. Washington sends a few more soldiers to bolster your defenses. He also sends Major General Israel Putnam to replace Greene, who has become too ill to command.

Major General Israel Putnam

Turn the page.

Putnam quickly plans a defense against a British attack. "Our main force will stay at the forts in Brooklyn Heights," he says. "And a smaller force will be sent to Guan Heights to defend the approach to our position."

He orders you to join those defending Guan Heights. On this part of Long Island, there are several routes that lead to Brooklyn Heights. The main one is Gowanus Road. It would be the easiest to take for a large force of soldiers. There is also the Jamaica Pass. This lesser-known path is not built for a large force. While everyone expects the British to use the Gowanus Road, you wonder if they might sneak down the Jamaica Pass. Which do you tell Putnam that you will defend?

To defend Gowanus Road, turn to page 30.
To defend Jamaica Pass, turn to page 34.

"We should keep to your original plan," you tell Washington. "Keep our main force on Manhattan. It's where the British will most likely attack."

Washington agrees. But he does send a few more troops to Long Island along with Major General Israel Putnam. Putnam replaces Greene who is too ill to remain in command.

What happens next takes even Washington by surprise. Early in the morning of August 27, the British launch their offensive—not against Manhattan as you suspected. Instead, they attack colonial positions on Long Island. The number of Redcoats on the island is nearly double what was initially reported. And the colonial soldiers are quickly pushed back to the forts in Brooklyn Heights.

Turn the page.

Washington is angry at his mistake. The British fooled him. But he is also worried about the thousands of troops on Long Island. Their backs are to the East River, and they are surrounded on three sides by a large British force.

"They won't be able to hold out long," Washington says. "And if they are captured, we lose a third of our forces. The Continental Army might never recover."

The colonists could even lose the war!

The soldiers on Long Island are trapped. You can think of two possible ways for them to escape. Washington could send more troops for them to fight their way out. If they win, they would also keep the British from landing troops on Manhattan.

Or Washington could order a retreat. New York will be lost, and it will be a big loss for the colonists. But the Continental Army will remain intact and be able to fight another day.

To send more troops to Brooklyn Heights, turn to page 36.
To retreat from Long Island, turn to page 38.

Of the roads leading to Brooklyn Heights, the Gowanus Road is probably the easiest one to march a large force down. It's the one you decide to help defend.

On August 27, you and about 1,600 men are guarding the pass when a force of Redcoats marches on your positions. Cannons boom and bullets whiz through the air. The fighting is fierce. You are outnumbered and have to give ground.

The Delaware Regiment bravely defended one of the main routes to the American forts in Brooklyn Heights.

As you fall back, you are surprised by a large British force coming from the east. That is the direction of the Jamaica Pass. The main contingent of British soldiers must have marched down the pass you did not defend. Now you are in danger of being surrounded by them.

Luckily, a small group of soldiers, later known as the Maryland 400, saves the day. They fight off the British while you retreat back to Brooklyn Heights.

Throughout the rest of the day, you hear the echo of musket fire off in the distance. More and more troops retreat back to Brooklyn Heights as the fighting continues.

From the stories you hear, you determine that Washington was wrong. Howe did not plan to attack Manhattan. Instead, he sent nearly 20,000 troops to Long Island. That is easily twice your number.

Turn the page.

By the end of the day, you see British soldiers digging in outside the fort's wall. They have you surrounded on three sides, and your backs are to the East River. It is only a matter of time before they attack.

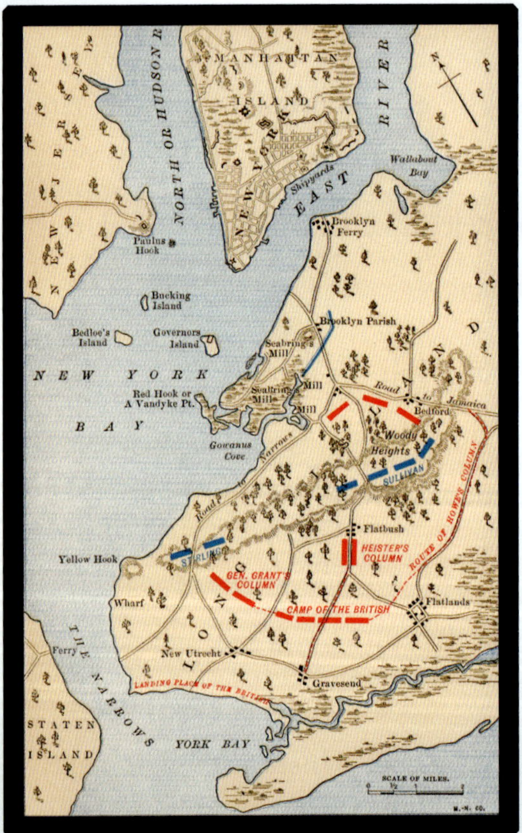

A map showing the positions of the Continental (blue) and British (red) armies during the Battle of Long Island

Putnam says to his officers, "If we are forced to surrender, much of the Continental Army will be lost—maybe even the war!"

"We need to ask Washington for more troops," an officer says.

"We need to retreat," another officer says.

Putnam puts you in charge of passing along a message to Washington. Do you ask him for reinforcements? More troops might help you hold the fort. But if you lose the battle, the war could be lost.

Or do you ask to retreat? You would lose New York. But even with reinforcements, you're not sure if you could hold Long Island for long.

To ask Washington for more troops, turn to page 36.
To ask Washington to retreat, turn to page 38.

"The British could use the Jamaica Pass," you say. "They might think we will leave it undefended."

"I doubt they even know of that route," Putnam says. "And I don't want to waste many troops defending it."

He assigns you and just a handful of soldiers to keep an eye on the pass.

But what Putnam doesn't know is that Loyalists told the British about this secret route to Brooklyn Heights. They help guide British forces down the narrow pass.

You and the troops with you are caught by surprise. You try to flee to warn your fellow soldiers, but you are taken prisoner. After that, all you hear are rumors of the battle. You learn the British force that marched down the Jamaica Pass overwhelmed colonial positions.

General Henry Clinton was in charge of marching British troops through the poorly guarded Jamaica Pass.

Your heart sinks. Long Island is lost, and so is New York City. You just hope that Washington escaped with enough of the Continental Army to continue the fight against the British.

THE END

To read another adventure, turn to page 11.

To learn more about Revolutionary War escapes, turn to page 101.

"We need to send more troops," you tell Washington. "If we lose Brooklyn Heights, we lose the city."

At first, Washington agrees. On August 28, he sends 1,500 troops across the East River. But as the British prepare for their attack, the general changes his mind.

"We can't hold New York. The British forces are just too great," he admits to his advisors. "We have to retreat or risk losing a third of our army."

On August 29, Washington makes a daring decision. He orders all available boats to sail to Brooklyn Heights. Under the cover of darkness, these boats carry some 9,000 troops from Long Island to Manhattan. They retreat undetected.

The next morning, the British are surprised to discover that the American forces have left their defenses.

Meanwhile, Washington marches his forces north. New York is lost. But at least the Continental Army escaped Howe's trap. If it hadn't, it might have been an even bigger defeat. The fight for freedom could have ended.

None of that changes Washington's sour mood. Mistakes were made during the Battle of Long Island. You feel Washington places some of the blame on you, even though you just agreed with his decisions. So it seems unfair when he sends you to Pennsylvania to report on events instead of staying at his side.

While you continue to serve in the Continental Army, Washington never asks you to serve alongside him again.

THE END

To read another adventure, turn to page 11.
To learn more about Revolutionary War escapes, turn to page 101.

"We can't win this battle," you tell Washington. "And if we lose a large portion of our army, we won't be able to win the war."

At first, Washington doesn't seem to agree with you. On August 28, he sends more than a thousand troops across the East River.

But as the British prepare for their attack, the general changes his mind.

"You're right," he admits. "We could lose more than New York if we don't retreat."

Washington's retreat from Long Island

On August 29, Washington plans a daring escape. He orders all the boats in the area to sail to Brooklyn Heights. Under the cover of darkness, these boats carry some 9,000 troops from Long Island to Manhattan. They escape undetected, and the Continental Army is saved.

The next few days and weeks are grueling as the army marches west toward Philadelphia. Soldiers are discouraged by the defeat at the Battle of Long Island. But you know that just like the victory at Boston did not win the war, this loss will not lose it. The fight for independence has just begun. And because of the part you played in saving the troops on Long Island, you proudly serve as one of Washington's most trusted advisors throughout the war.

THE END

To read another adventure, turn to page 11.

To learn more about Revolutionary War escapes, turn to page 101.

The HMS *Royal George* of the British Royal Navy had 100 guns on three decks.

CHAPTER 3

SAILING AS A PRIVATEER

For you, sailing is a part of life. You enjoy smelling the salty breeze and hearing the crash of breaking waves along the shoreline. You practically live on the water, whether aboard a small fishing sloop or a large merchant ship. It is only natural that you are interested in serving as a sailor when war breaks out.

At this time, Great Britain's Royal Navy is the most powerful in the world. It has hundreds of ships, including large 100-gun battleships. The colonies do not even have a navy. Up until now, their ships relied on the Royal Navy for protection. They had no need for warships. But all that is quickly changing.

Turn the page.

You know ships are the quickest and easiest way to move troops and supplies to where they are needed. General George Washington understands this as well. As commander of the Continental Army, he takes command of several ships during the summer of 1775. They are used to prevent British ships from transporting troops and supplies.

Under Washington's urging, the Second Continental Congress establishes the Continental Navy in the fall of 1775. Esek Hopkins is placed in command of the navy and is eventually given the rank of admiral.

Commander Esek Hopkins

By the spring of 1776, the Continental Navy has only a handful of ships—not nearly enough to challenge the Royal Navy. Then you hear that Congress has decided to allow privateering. Captains of fishing boats and merchant ships are given permission to arm their vessels and attack British ships. You are excited about this news. As a sailor, it is your best chance to join the Patriots' fight for freedom against Great Britain.

Being a privateer is kind of like being a pirate. You will be attacking British ships and taking their cargo. While that sounds like piracy, which is against the law, there is one big difference. Congress is allowing colonial captains to attack British ships, which makes it lawful.

This adds hundreds of vessels and thousands of sailors to fight. You are among those sailors. But what type of ship are you serving aboard when the war breaks out?

Turn the page.

If it's a small fishing sloop, you'll keep to the colonies' coastal waters during your service. Sloops can be fast and stealthy but are not built for carrying large artillery.

If you're aboard a large merchant ship, you'll sail out in the open ocean. Merchant ships can be outfitted with rows of cannons and used to battle other ships.

To serve aboard a fishing vessel, go to page 45.
To serve aboard a merchant ship, turn to page 48.

American privateers during the Revolutionary War

When the war breaks out, you are serving aboard a fishing sloop. Your captain outfits his ship with a couple small swivel cannons. The sloop can safely travel in coastal waters, but it's not built for long voyages. Also, you don't have the firepower to challenge the bigger ships you might come across in the open ocean. Your captain likes to stay close to his fishing grounds off Nantucket. He harasses any British ship that seems like easy prey.

Turn the page.

One night, you spy a British sloop anchored near shore. From where you are, you see only a handful of sailors aboard the small ship. While there are British warships farther out in the bay, this smaller ship is a prize your captain does not want to pass up.

"We could add that sloop to our fleet," he tells you. "And if we are quiet and quick about it, we'll be sailing off before those warships get wind of us."

It sounds risky, but the colonists need to take risks to defeat the mighty Royal Navy. Your captain sends men out in boats. You quietly tug at the oars, thankful you are not spotted by the time you reach the sloop. Then you scamper up its sides. All is going well as the sailors with you scatter across the deck.

But suddenly a shot rings out. There is yelling. You hear men struggling with one of the crew. Another shot is fired.

Then you hear fearful news from one of your men. "Those warships have dropped boats in the water," he says.

You look over the railing. Sure enough, you see lanterns from about a dozen boats headed in your direction.

You have a choice to make. You could keep fighting for control of the ship. If the battle is quick, you will be underway before the British reach you. Or you could attempt to flee. As long as you outrow the British, you should be able to get away safely and out of range of their muskets.

To continue fighting, turn to page 50.
To flee, turn to page 53.

When the war breaks out, you are serving aboard a three-masted merchant ship carrying cargo between the colonies and Europe. But that changes when the fighting starts. It has suddenly become much more dangerous for colonial ships to be out in the open ocean. Also, your captain is a Patriot and supports the colonists in their fight for freedom.

As soon as Congress allows privateering, he outfits his ship with more than 20 cannons. While it's no match for a British warship, you have the firepower to challenge most merchant ships.

Since your captain usually sails between the colonies and Great Britain, he is given a Letter of Marque from Congress. This document gives him authority to capture British merchant ships wherever he might come across them.

The northern Atlantic is your hunting ground. You sail back and forth across the ocean. If you spot a British warship, you run. If you spy a British merchant ship, you give chase. It's a daring life, but you find it much more exciting than working as a merchant.

One day, you spy sails in the distance. It is a one-masted British sloop. It could be a perfect target for your crew. But as you approach, the ship turns its broadside to you, and you see a bank of cannons.

The sloop does not have as much firepower as you. You could still try to take it. Capturing even a small warship would be a worthy prize. But you would be facing a Royal Navy ship. Its sailors are well-trained for battle, unlike the crew you sail with. Maybe it would be better to flee.

To attack, turn to page 55.
To flee, turn to page 57.

Sure, you likely could outrow the approaching British boats. You might even escape the sailors' musket fire. But those warships and their cannons would be another matter. They won't fire upon you while aboard one of their own ships. But out in your rowboats, you won't be so lucky.

You need to win the sloop—and quick! Only that turns out to be more difficult than you had hoped. Random shots are fired. There is cursing and grunting as combatants fight hand to hand. You hear the splash of a man going overboard. In the chaos, you don't know if it's one of yours or one of theirs.

Then, as you are wrestling with a sailor, you hear someone shout, "Stop, or I'll fire!"

You turn to see a British sailor standing over you. He's one of the sailors who rowed over from the warships.

The fight took too long, and now it is lost.

The rest of your men are quickly rounded up. By the time the battle is over, there are only a handful left.

You are thankful the British don't consider you a pirate. Otherwise, they would have you hanged. Instead, you are taken prisoner. You are placed below deck on a small ship with a dozen other prisoners. You are all being sent to New York.

On the way, you hear one of the prisoners whisper, "There aren't many guards aboard this ship. Together, we could take them."

"Thomas, hush," another prisoner replies. "Talk like that will get you shot."

"What about you?" Thomas asks, turning to you. "Would you help ol' Thomas Painter out of the fix he's in?"

Turn the page.

You have an idea of what's ahead. Once in New York, you will be locked aboard a prison ship. Escape will be near impossible. And the conditions will be horrible. You will be lucky not to die of disease or starvation before the war is over. It's not a fate you look forward to. But looking around the group of prisoners, each one seems in worse shape than the next. They are tired and hungry. You doubt any of them would be up for a fight if you tried to escape.

To agree to help Thomas, turn to page 60.
To turn down Thomas's request for help, turn to page 62.

You don't know if you have time to take the ship before the British boats reach you. It's best to flee so you can fight another day.

"To the boats!" you shout.

All around you, men leap over the railings and crawl into the boats. As you row away, musket fire comes from the remaining British sailors aboard the sloop. Shots are fired from the British boats rowing toward you.

Musket balls whiz through the air. But in the dark, you're a hard target to hit.

Then you hear a loud boom off in the distance.

"One of the warships is firing cannons at us!" a sailor yells.

Turn the page.

A cannonball doesn't need to hit you to be dangerous. One bursts close to your small boat. The explosion tosses you into the water, and your world goes black as you hit your head against something wooden. Unconscious, you sink to the bottom of the ocean.

THE END

To read another adventure, turn to page 11.

To learn more about Revolutionary War escapes, turn to page 101.

A three-masted frigate

The ship you are facing is smaller than your three-masted merchant ship, and you have more cannons.

"We can take her, Captain," you say.

"Aye, then let's give her a fight," the captain says.

Sailors scramble to their positions. Some rush to load the cannons. Others set to work in the rigging.

Turn the page.

"Turn us about!" the captain orders.

The helmsman turns the wheel. You feel the ship change direction so that you have a bank of cannons facing the enemy ship.

But the British already have their cannons aimed in your direction. You hear a series of booms. Cannonballs rip through your sails. They crash into your hull, sending splintering wood in all directions.

You feel a sudden, sharp pain. A large piece of shrapnel has struck you in the chest. You collapse to the deck and realize your adventures have ended.

THE END

To read another adventure, turn to page 11.

To learn more about Revolutionary War escapes, turn to page 101.

While you think you could easily capture a poorly armed merchant vessel, a warship would be much more difficult. Even a small one. British sailors are well-trained, and your crew has little battle experience.

"We're no match for her, Captain," you say.

"Aye, best we run!" the captain yells to his crew.

The helmsman turns the ship, and sailors leap to action in the rigging. Behind you, the British ship changes course to follow you. You've quickly gone from hunter to prey. Now the chase is on.

But your large merchant ship is not built for speed. Even with the wind filling your sails, the British warship eventually pulls alongside you.

Turn the page.

A cannon is fired and splashes just off your prow. It is a warning shot. Sure, you could arm your cannons and fight back, but your captain does not like the odds.

"I'd like to live to see the end of this war," he says.

He surrenders his ship to the British. The crew is taken prisoner.

Days later, you find yourself aboard the prison ship HMS *Jersey*. It is anchored off the coast of New York City. The prison ship is much larger than the merchant ship you served aboard, and you are just one of hundreds of prisoners.

The conditions on the prison ship are horrible. The food is poor, and illnesses ravage your fellow prisoners. One day, a couple prisoners approach you.

The HMS *Jersey* prison ship anchored near Long Island

"My name's Christopher Hawkins," one says. "And we're planning an escape. Would you like to join us?"

You know it'd be risky. The ship is far from shore, and there are armed guards always watching you. But you also don't know how you will survive these conditions until the end of the war. Your captain has already died of illness.

To join the escape plan, turn to page 65.
To turn down the escape plan, turn to page 66.

"I'm with you," you tell Thomas.

Then you two work on a plan. Thomas will convince more sailors to join in the escape attempt. You will distract the guards.

You decide the right moment is when the guards bring you food. They will have their hands full, giving you a chance to run up on deck. That will also give your fellow prisoners their opportunity to attack.

Your part goes as planned. When the guards come in carrying food, you rush past them. They are momentarily confused.

"Hey!" one of them yells as you rush up on deck.

But that's where the plan falls apart. None of the other prisoners rise up to attack. Thomas must have failed to convince them.

That doesn't matter to you now. Looking around, you don't see any guards on deck. You still have a chance to escape. You leap over the railing and into the water. You start to swim away.

You hear shouts yelling after you. Still, you keep swimming.

You hear muskets being fired.

Then you feel a sharp pain and your world goes black.

THE END

To read another adventure, turn to page 11.
To learn more about Revolutionary War escapes, turn to page 101.

"Doesn't matter how many guards there are," you reply. "No one here looks fit to fight."

Thomas grumbles at that, but he seems to admit it's best not to try anything. At least not now.

Upon reaching New York, you are placed aboard the prison ship HMS *Good Hope*. It is anchored in the East River. During the day, you are allowed a small amount of freedom, though guards are always watching you. At night, you are locked below deck with a guard outside the door.

American Patriots were crammed into prison ships with little food and no hope of escape.

The conditions are horrible. The food is poor, and it seems like every few days someone falls ill. You wonder if you should have taken up Thomas's offer to escape.

One day, you catch him staring at a boat tied to the ship's anchor line. It's kept there for whenever the British sailors need to go ashore.

"If we grabbed a couple oars, maybe we could get away," Thomas whispers to you.

"But what about the guards?" you ask. "They'd catch or shoot us before we got near shore."

"We just need to make friends with a couple of them," he says with a smile, "and distract them."

"How?" you ask.

Turn the page.

He explains his plan. Every night, the prisoners get a small ration of rum to drink. He will save his rations. Then one night he'll share all he's saved with the guards.

"That should do the trick," he says.

Earlier, you said no to helping Thomas. Do you think this plan is any better? There are risks no matter what you decide. An escape attempt could have deadly consequences. Then again, staying aboard the prison ship longer increases your chances of falling ill like many of your fellow prisoners.

To go along with Thomas's plan, turn to page 67.
To say no to helping Thomas, turn to page 69.

With the poor conditions aboard the ship, you believe staying is just as dangerous as attempting to escape. And you would rather risk an escape than wait for an illness to kill you.

"I'll join," you say.

"Good to have you with us," Christopher says.

Then he explains the first part of his plan. You need to get some tools to loosen the bars of your cell. But where will you get them? Up on deck, you know where some large tools like axes and shovels are stored. But with the guards on deck, that might be risky. Or you could sneak into the galley below deck. It is less likely you would be seen, but you don't know if there would be any useful tools.

To search for tools up on the deck, turn to page 71.
To search for tools in the galley, turn to page 73.

The risk of attempting an escape seems too great. You can't imagine swimming all the way to shore without getting caught or—worse—shot! You decide not to join the group.

Then one night, the prisoners you had talked to suddenly disappear. You learn that they stole an axe from the galley and used it to work loose the bars of their cell. They left the ship and swam for shore.

You never hear what happen to them. But you like to imagine they made it to freedom. The idea that they escaped is one of the things that keeps your spirits up as you wait for your release at the end of the war.

THE END

To read another adventure, turn to page 11.
To learn more about Revolutionary War escapes, turn to page 101.

"I'm in," you tell Thomas.

It's either escape or risk dying from disease and starvation aboard the ship.

Thomas finds a discarded bottle. Every night, you two pour your rations of rum into the bottle. You do this until Thomas feels you have enough to tempt the guards.

Then one night, he calls over to the guard at the door. "I've got a little something here for you, if you let us up on deck tonight."

The guard smiles at the bottle Thomas holds up. He unlocks the door and lets you up on deck. While Thomas pours rum for the guards, you find two oars for the boat.

Soon, more prisoners sneak up on deck. The commotion grows. As the guards enjoy the rum, some prisoners start to sneak off—lowering themselves into the water.

Turn the page.

"It's time to go," Thomas whispers in your ear, "before someone sounds the alarm."

You slip into the water, and Thomas hands you one of the oars. Then you feel the water's current take hold. It pulls you downriver, away from the boat.

The plan was for you and Thomas to escape aboard the boat. To do that, you will need two oars. That means you will need to fight the river's current and hope both of you can reach the boat. Or you could let the river's current carry you away. Swimming may not be as fast as escaping aboard the boat. But it'll be a much quieter getaway.

To swim for the boat, turn to page 75.
To swim away, turn to page 77.

This plan sounds more dangerous than the last one. You can't imagine it working.

"I'm out," you say. "I don't want to risk getting shot trying to escape."

But that doesn't stop Thomas. He finds another partner. You see them pouring their rations of rum into a discarded bottle they found. Then one night, you wake to a commotion. Your cell door is unlocked. You join the prisoners rushing up on deck. Some are leaping into the water, and others stand about confused. Before you can decide what to do, rough hands grab you and force you back below deck.

"Back where you belong," a guard shouts.

Before the night is out, most of the prisoners are fished out of the water and thrown below deck with you. But you notice a few are missing. One of them is Thomas.

Turn the page.

You wonder if he got away or if he was shot escaping. But you never hear what happened to him.

Shortly after Thomas's escape, you start feeling feverish. Then you notice a rash on your arms and legs. It's smallpox. You missed your chance to escape, and now you've caught a deadly disease.

THE END

To read another adventure, turn to page 11.
To learn more about Revolutionary War escapes, turn to page 101.

You figure sneaking up on deck is your best chance to find the tools you'll need.

Christopher agrees but then says, "I'll check the galley, though. Maybe I'll get lucky."

One day, you head your separate ways. For the most part, the guards don't pay you much attention. While it's light out, anyone attempting to swim to shore would be seen and easily caught. At night, prisoners are locked below deck.

You find a couple axes. But you never thought about how you would carry them without looking suspicious. You quickly catch the attention of a guard.

Turn the page.

“Hey, what are you doing?” he shouts.

After the guard sees the axes you are carrying, he sends you back below deck. From then on, you have a guard watching you at all times. You are not able to talk to Christopher again. Worse, you are not able to sneak off with him when his escapes.

You’re left aboard the prison ship hoping the war ends before you catch a deadly disease.

THE END

To read another adventure, turn to page 11.
To learn more about Revolutionary War escapes, turn to page 101.

"It's too risky to go up on deck," you say.

So one day, you and Christopher sneak into the galley. There you find a small axe that you hide under your shirt and sneak back to your cell. Another member of your crew finds a crowbar.

The next part of the plan is tricky. You need to loosen the bars of your cell so you can sneak out of it. Christopher has you wait for a stormy night. Every time thunder booms, you chop at the wood around the bars. The sound of the storm hides what you are doing and keeps the guards from getting suspicious.

On a calm night, Christopher has you loosen the bars of your cell. One by one, you all sneak out and slip into the water.

You dive down and swim underwater as far as you can. When you come back to the surface, you are beyond the lantern light from the ship.

Turn the page.

The HMS *Jersey* could hold more than 1,000 prisoners.

Using the dark to your advantage, you swim to shore. You go slow to avoid making any sounds that might alert the guards.

When you reach the beach, you are cold and exhausted. But you're happy to have escaped the horrible conditions aboard the *Jersey*.

THE END

To read another adventure, turn to page 11.
To learn more about Revolutionary War escapes, turn to page 101.

You need that boat to make a quick escape. You swim toward it. It's not easy with an oar in one hand. All your splashing makes a lot of noise.

By the time you reach the boat, you're exhausted. But that's not the worst of it. You don't see Thomas anywhere. The current must have carried him away.

With only one oar, the boat is almost useless to you. You think about untying it and letting it drift away.

But before you can act, one of the guards yells, "There's another one! He's aboard the boat! After him!"

You're caught! To try to escape now would put you at risk of getting shot. So you wait until a couple guards pull the boat back to the ship. They haul you up and lock you below deck with a few other cold and wet prisoners.

Turn the page.

You failed to escape. Now you need to hope you can survive the rest of the war without getting deathly ill.

THE END

To read another adventure, turn to page 11.

To learn more about Revolutionary War escapes, turn to page 101.

Fighting the current with an oar in hand would be a struggle. A struggle that would make a lot of noise as you splash around in the water. You decide to let the river carry you away. The oar does come in handy, though. It helps you keep afloat.

Thomas must have done the same. You hear someone else swimming near to you. But you do not want to call out and risk the guards aboard the ship hearing you.

So you let yourself drift downriver. This will not be the end of your journey. You are behind enemy lines and will need to find a way back home. But at least you have escaped the prison ship.

THE END

To read another adventure, turn to page 11.
To learn more about Revolutionary War escapes, turn to page 101.

The Battle of Saratoga was a decisive victory for the Continental Army that resulted in the surrender of General Burgoyne's army.

CHAPTER 4
RUNNING WITH THE SWAMP FOX

Early in the war, you aren't involved in the fighting. Most of the battles occur in the northern colonies while you live in the south. But you hear of the defeat at the Battle of Long Island in 1776, the first major battle of the war. You also celebrate the Patriots' victory at the Battle of Trenton in New Jersey. It is considered the Continental Army's first major victory.

Things begin to change in 1777. The French offer their support to the colonists, and the British suffer a major defeat at the Battle of Saratoga in New York. Because of this, the British turn their attention south, to where you live.

Turn the page.

The British believe many Loyalists live in the southern colonies. Unlike you and other Patriots, these colonists remain loyal to British rule. The British hope these Loyalists will help them gain control of the southern colonies.

You worry as the British Southern Strategy gets under way. Late in 1778, they capture the port city of Savannah, Georgia. Then Charleston, South Carolina, falls to the British early in 1780.

By this time, you are an officer serving under the command of Major General Horatio Gates. He's been charged with winning the south back from the British. He begins by setting his sights on Camden, South Carolina. It's a major supply depot for the British. Taking the city could cripple the British war effort.

On the march, you are met by Lieutenant Colonel Francis Marion. He and Gates discuss the upcoming battle. Gates will continue toward Camden with roughly 3,000 troops. Gates sends Marion with a group of men to attack British supply lines.

You have the choice of joining either one. You could continue on with Gates toward Camden. That would give you the chance to fight in the first major battle of his campaign. It could likely decide the outcome of the war in the south.

Or you could join Marion on his raid. Like General Washington, he fought during the French and Indian War. You've also heard rumors about his successful raids against the British.

To go with Gates, turn to page 82.
To go with Marion, turn to page 85.

Major General Horatio Gates

You decide to stay with Gates. The battle ahead will be an important one. If Gates wins, it will be a major step in stopping the British from taking over the south.

On August 15, after you finish your evening meal, Gates orders a night march. He wants to be in position early the next morning. You come across British troops about 5 miles from Camden.

The British forces number just over 2,000, which include Loyalist troops. You like your odds, but it is experience that often decides battles. Many of Gates's troops are untrained militia, while the Redcoats are professional soldiers.

When the fighting starts, the difference is clear. A volley of British musket fire sends many of Gates's militia fleeing without ever having fired a shot.

The battle is quickly lost. You hold your position to allow Gates to escape, but you are captured and taken prisoner along with more than 100 other soldiers. The British march you toward Charleston where you will likely be placed aboard a prison ship until the war ends.

One night, while you are resting after the day's long march, you hear musket fire. A couple British soldiers fall. Others grab their muskets.

Turn the page.

Francis Marion

Before the British soldiers can return fire, you see a familiar face charging into your camp. Marion has come to rescue you.

Marion gives you a choice. One option is to return home. After the horrible loss at the Battle of Camden, many of the soldiers taken prisoner with you believe the war in the south is now lost. The other option is to join Marion's small band in fighting the British. But it will be risky because they are greatly outnumbered.

To go home, turn to page 87.
To join Marion, turn to page 88.

You are impressed by the rumors you've heard about Marion. He hasn't won any major battles, but he has fought in several minor skirmishes. He is a cunning leader known for harassing the Redcoats at every opportunity.

You follow him to Port's Ferry, an important crossing over the Pee Dee River. By capturing it, you will cut off a British supply line to Camden.

On August 15, you sneak up on the crossing. There is a small force of Loyalists defending it. From your hiding spots, you fire at them with your muskets and quickly run them off.

The next day, you hear that the battle at Camden was a major defeat. Gates's forces are in disarray, and many soldiers were taken prisoner.

"I bet the British will take any prisoners to Charleston," Marion says. "I believe they have prison ships there."

Turn the page.

Marion leads his band toward Charleston. One night you come across a camp of British soldiers. They are guarding more than 100 colonial prisoners. They look like they were part of the forces who attacked Camden.

Marion positions his men in the trees surrounding the British. The attack is quick and fierce. You charge into the camp, firing your musket. The British hardly have a chance to put up a fight.

This tends to be the way Marion harasses the British. He engages in guerrilla warfare. His strikes are quick, and then he usually retreats before taking many casualties.

Turn to page 89.

Most of the other prisoners decide against joining Marion. They believe that the defeat at Camden is too much for the colonists to overcome, and you do too. Instead of continuing the fight for freedom, you head home.

Over the coming months, you hear rumors about Marion. He becomes known as the Swamp Fox for the way he evades capture. Also, with his guerrilla warfare tactics, he harasses the British. He defeats Loyalist forces, and his efforts help change the tide of the war in the south.

By the time the colonists win their freedom, he has been promoted to Brigadier General. He is known as one of the great heroes of the war. If only you had decided to fight alongside him, you too would be considered a hero.

THE END

To read another adventure, turn to page 11.
To learn more about Revolutionary War escapes, turn to page 101.

Many of the prisoners do not take Marion up on his offer. They feel that the war has been lost after the defeat at Camden. Yet you still have hope. You want to continue fighting. So you join his small band.

Before joining Marion, you were used to battles being fought with armies lining up out in the open to face each other. They would exchange volley after volley of musket fire.

But Marion uses different tactics. With his small force, he can't afford to battle out in the open. Instead, he engages in guerrilla warfare. He makes quick strikes against the British and then retreats before taking many casualties.

Go to the next page.

Francis Marion used surprise attacks to harass the Loyalists and the British.

Marion puts his tactics on display for you at the Battle of Blue Savannah. He heard that a force of Loyalists were marching toward him. Even though he is outnumbered, he goes on the attack.

Marion marches toward the Loyalist camp. But when a large force blocks your path, he orders a retreat.

Turn the page.

This is all part of the plan. You run and hide in Blue Savannah, a low-lying area with small pine trees for cover. The Loyalists follow. When they are in range, Marion yells, "Charge!"

You rush out firing muskets. The surprised Loyalists fire wildly and then turn to flee.

While it's a small victory, it's a big loss for the Loyalist forces in the area. Marion helps end their threat against the Patriots.

Throughout the summer of 1780, you fight alongside Marion. He continues to harass British forces with his guerrilla attacks. His success turns him into a folk hero among the Patriots. But he draws the attention of the British army's leaders.

In the fall of that year, Marion learns that British Lieutenant Colonel Banastre Tarleton has been assigned to hunt him down. You wonder what Marion will do to escape being captured.

Not long after, Marion hears rumors of Tarleton's location. He is believed to be heading toward Singleton's Mill.

Marion discusses his options with you. He could march on Tarleton's location and try to trick the British officer like he tricked the Loyalists during the Battle of Blue Savannah. Though, facing poorly trained Loyalist soldiers is much less risky than well-trained Redcoats. Or he could try to lead Tarleton into a trap. Nelson's Ferry is about 30 miles from Singleton's Mill. Marion could wait for Tarleton to chase after him and set up an ambush there.

To attack Tarleton at Singleton's Mill, turn to page 92.
To ambush Tarleton at Nelson's Ferry, turn to page 94.

"What we did during the Battle of Blue Savannah worked on the Loyalists," you tell Marion.

He thinks for a moment and then shakes his head.

"But this time we'll be up against professional soldiers," he explains. "The Redcoats won't be so easily scared off, and Tarleton is too good a leader to fall for that trick."

Francis Marion and his men camp and plan their next attacks.

"But if we defeat Tarleton, that would be a major victory for us," you say.

Marion isn't convinced. In the end, he decides he can't risk confronting the British. Not this time. Instead, Marion flees.

It's upsetting to you. You find it cowardly and decide to leave Marion's small band. But over the final years of the war, you hear more of Marion's exploits.

It turns out his decision to flee and fight another day was likely the best choice. In the end, he becomes a hero among the colonists for all of his small victories against the British.

THE END

To read another adventure, turn to page 11.
To learn more about Revolutionary War escapes, turn to page 101.

"We can't risk confronting Tarleton head on," you say. "It's best to plan an ambush for him. Maybe we can catch the British off guard."

Marion agrees, and you march to Nelson's Ferry. You take up a position in the area and wait in ambush.

But Tarleton never appears.

"Maybe he suspected an ambush," you say.

Marion nods in agreement.

"But that also gives us an opportunity," Marion says. "If Tarleton thinks we are camped here, maybe we can sneak up on him."

From people in the area, you hear various rumors. One says that Tarleton sent his main force back to Camden. Also, you hear of British patrols fleeing the area. Then someone tells you of a fire at the Richardsons' plantation.

Do you tell Marion to check out the fire? The Richardsons are a well-known Patriot family. They could be in danger. From the news you've been hearing, it sounds like the British forces have abandoned their chase. So it should be safe.

Or do you tell Marion that this might be a trap? That maybe the rumors aren't true? Maybe Tarleton set the fire to lure Marion into an ambush?

To help the Richardsons, turn to page 96.
To say it's a trap, turn to page 98.

"We must help them," you say. "The Richardsons are Patriots who support our cause. It's our duty!"

"I wish it were that easy," Marion tells you. "But I feel this is a ruse to lure us into a trap."

You go on to remind Marion of the rumors that Tarleton's main force has returned to Camden. You tell him of the British soldiers fleeing the area. But none of that convinces him.

So you decide to set out on your own. You want to make sure the Richardsons are safe.

After making the march to their house, you find that it's not the house that is on fire. A large bonfire has been set by someone.

You also find several British muskets aimed at you. You are quickly taken prisoner and questioned about Marion's location. You refuse to say anything.

Lieutenant Colonel Banastre Tarleton

Tarleton isn't impressed by your lack of cooperation. He sends you to Charleston. There you will be locked aboard a prison ship until the end of the war.

THE END

To read another adventure, turn to page 11.
To learn more about Revolutionary War escapes, turn to page 101.

"It all seems too easy," you tell Marion.

"Just like a trap," Marion says.

Marion decides to be cautious. Instead of sending his forces in to attack, he scouts out the Richardsons' plantation. What he finds is Richard Richardson Jr. sneaking away.

"It's a trap," Richard warns. "Tarleton has artillery set up around the farm, and hundreds of men are hiding in the surrounding woods waiting for you."

Hearing that, Marion knows this is not a fight he can win. Instead of continuing their game of cat-and-mouse, he decides to flee. Marion marches his band of men over rivers and through bogs.

Tarleton hears news of this and gives chase. But Marion knows the land better than the British. He escapes into the Ox Swamp.

Upon reaching the swamp, Tarleton gives up the chase. He realizes he could never catch the Patriot leader.

Later you hear rumors that Tarleton cursed, "As for [that] old fox, the Devil himself could not catch him."

That rumor, combined with his cunning, help Marion earn the nickname the Swamp Fox. And because of his escape, Marion is able to continue his guerrilla warfare against British forces. You are also able to continue fighting by his side. Thanks to joining his small band of soldiers, you take part in skirmishes that help the colonists eventually defeat the British.

THE END

To read another adventure, turn to page 11.
To learn more about Revolutionary War escapes, turn to page 101.

British troops surrendered after Washington's army defeated them at Yorktown.

CHAPTER 5

END OF THE WAR

The Revolutionary War ended in victory for the colonists when they defeated the British at the Battle of Yorktown in Virginia in 1781. British General Cornwallis surrendered to General Washington. The war officially ended a couple years later with the signing of the Treaty of Paris in 1783.

It was a long, hard fight for freedom. More than 30,000 members of the Continental Army were killed, wounded, or taken prisoner. Thousands more died from illness while serving, and many who were captured also died from disease and the harsh conditions of their confinement.

Along the way, there were many tales of heroism and brave escapes—none more important than what happened during the Battle of Long Island. Leading up to his final retreat, General Washington made the wrong choice to defend Manhattan over Long Island. This decision nearly cost the colonists the war. In the end, about 2,000 colonial troops were killed, wounded, or captured. But his daring decision to sneak soldiers across the East River in the middle of the night was the right choice. By escaping the British, he kept the Continental Army intact.

The Continental Army loads cannons on a boat during the retreat from Long Island.

HMS *Jersey*

During the war, most colonial soldiers who were imprisoned were held aboard prison ships like the HMS *Jersey*. This large, retired warship could hold more than 1,000 prisoners. Keeping prisoners on a ship made escape nearly impossible. Escapees had to swim to reach shore, sometimes in bitterly cold water. It was easy to spot and recapture them while they were swimming.

But there were rare stories of people who made daring escapes, such as Thomas Painter and Christopher Hawkins. Painter saved up his nightly ration of rum to distract the guards and make an escape. Hawkins used an axe he stole from the ship's galley. On stormy nights, as thunder boomed, he hacked an opening to escape from his cell.

Francis Marion's famous flight from British Lieutenant Colonel Banastre Tarleton was also a great escape. Before fleeing into the Ox Swamp, Marion played an important role in defeating Loyalist forces in the south. Afterward, he continued to harass British forces.

While Marion never took part in any large battles, his ability to escape capture and claim small victories helped the colonists take back the south from the British.

Francis Marion and his men on the run in a forest

It is because of leaders like Washington and Marion that the colonists won the war. If these brave heroes had not escaped the British, the war for independence could have ended very differently.

MAP OF THE 13 COLONIES

KEY EVENTS OF THE REVOLUTIONARY WAR

APRIL 19, 1775 The Battles of Lexington and Concord begin the Revolutionary War.

APRIL 1775 The Siege of Boston begins.

JUNE 1775 George Washington is given command of the Continental Army.

MARCH 1776 The Siege of Boston ends.

JULY 1776 The Declaration of Independence is adopted.

AUGUST 27–29, 1776 The Battle of Long Island is fought.

DECEMBER 26, 1776 The Battle of Trenton takes place.

SEPTEMBER 19–OCTOBER 7, 1777 The Battle of Saratoga is fought.

AUGUST 16, 1780 The Battle of Camden occurs.

SEPTEMBER 28–OCTOBER 19, 1781 The Battle of Yorktown takes place; the British surrender.

SEPTEMBER 3, 1783 The Treaty of Paris is signed; the war is officially over.

OTHER PATHS TO EXPLORE

- During the Battle of Long Island, General Washington escaped with the Continental Army intact. But what if that didn't happen? What if the nearly 9,000 troops on Long Island were captured? How would that change the war? Could the colonies still win? Would Washington remain in command of the army? Or would some other hero eventually become the first president of the United States?

- In Chapter 3, you try to escape from a British prison ship. But instead of being a prisoner yourself, what if you were trying to help someone who was imprisoned? How would you attempt to help a friend escape from the prison ship? How would you get to the ship anchored out in the river? How would you keep the guards from getting suspicious? And how would you break your friend out of their cell?

- In Chapter 4, you battle British Redcoats and Loyalists. But imagine that you are not a Patriot. Instead, you're among those colonists who support British rule. What would it be like being a Loyalist? What would it be like fighting alongside British Redcoats? Also, what might it be like living in the colonies after the British are defeated?

GLOSSARY

artillery (ar-TI-luhr-ee)—cannons and other large guns used during battles

casualty (KAZH-oo-uhl-tee)—someone who is injured, captured, killed, or missing in a disaster or a war

colony (KAH-luh-nee)—a place that is settled by people from another country and is controlled by that country

galley (GAL-ee)—place where sailors eat aboard a ship

merchant (MUR-chuhnt)—a person who buys and sells goods for profit

militia (muh-LISH-uh)—a group of citizens who are organized to fight, but who are not professional soldiers

plantation (plan-TAY-shuhn)—a large farm where crops such as cotton and sugarcane are grown; before 1865, plantations were run by slave labor

Redcoats (RED-coats)—British soldiers, named after the color of their uniforms

siege (SEEJ)—a military operation when an army surrounds the enemy and cuts off supplies

skirmish (SKUR-mish)—a small battle

sloop (SLOOP)—a sailboat with one mast and sails that are set from front to back

BIBLIOGRAPHY

Hawkins, Christopher. *The Adventures of Christopher Hawkins*. Hathi Trust Digital Library. March 17, 2023. catalog.hathitrust.org/Record/009596703.

Library of Congress. Map: Battle of Long Island. March 17, 2023. loc.gov/resource/g3802l.ct004118.

North Carolina Digital Collections. "Letter of Marque signed by John Hancock, 1776." March 17, 2023. digital.ncdcr.gov/digital/collection/p15012coll11/id/104.

Painter, Thomas. *Autobiography of Thomas Painter, Relating His Experiences During the War of the Revolution*. Internet Archive. March 17, 2023. archive.org/details/autobiographyoft00pain.

READ MORE

Braun, Eric. *The Real George Washington: The Truth Behind the Legend.* North Mankato, MN: Compass Point Books, 2019.

Kerry, Isaac. *The Battles of Lexington and Concord: A Day that Changed America.* North Mankato, MN: Capstone Press, 2023.

Smith, Elliott. *Hidden Heroes in the Revolutionary War.* Minneapolis: Lerner Publications, 2023.

INTERNET SITES

American Battlefield Trust—Brooklyn, New York
battlefields.org/learn/revolutionary-war/battles/brooklyn

History.com—The HMS Jersey
history.com/topics/american-revolution/the-hms-jersey

Smithsonian Magazine—The Swamp Fox
smithsonianmag.com/history/the-swamp-fox-157330429

ABOUT THE AUTHOR

photo by Russell Griesmer

Blake Hoena grew up in central Wisconsin, where he wrote stories about robots conquering the moon and trolls lumbering around the woods behind his parents' house. He now lives in Minnesota and enjoys writing about fun things like history, space aliens, and superheroes. Blake has written more than 50 chapter books and dozens of graphic novels for children.

BOOKS IN THIS SERIES